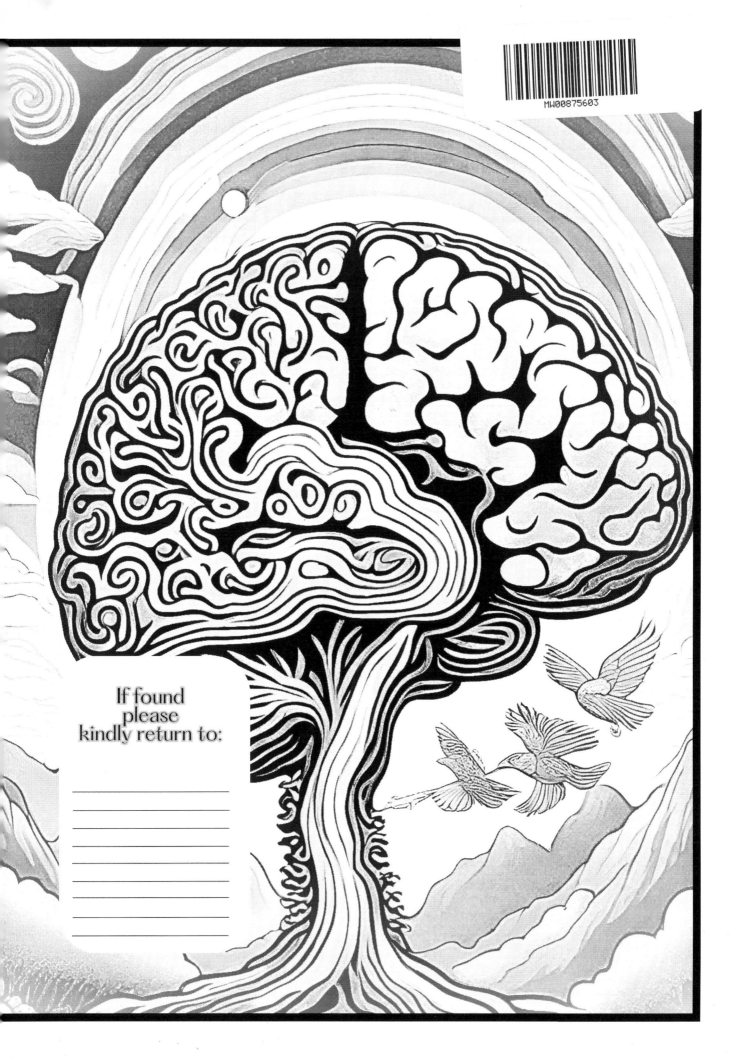

If found
please
kindly return to:

harmony mind renewal

A 10-DAY GUIDE TO MINDFULNESS FOR HEALING AND RESILIENCE

RAQUEL RENÉ MARTIN

Copyright

Harmony Mind Renewal
RQLRN
www.rqlrn.com

Published by RQLRN
First Edition, January 2024

ISBN: 000-0-0000000-0-0

Names: Martin, Raquel René, author and editor.
Title: Harmony Mind Renewal
Description: First Edition. | RQLRN 2024.
Identifiers: ISBN 000-0-0000000-0-0
Subjects: LCSH: Mindfulness (Psychology) | Meditation | Self-help techniques.
Classification: LCC BF0000.A1 D00 2024 | DDC 158.1—dc23

Cover design by Raquel René Martin
Interior design by Raquel René Martin
Illustrations by Raquel René Martin

Printed in the United States of America

First Edition

Dedication

To all the souls who have walked through the shadowed valleys of trauma:

May this book serve as a gentle companion on your journey toward healing.

To those who have faced the unimaginable, yet have found the courage to move forward, your resilience is a testament to the indomitable human spirit.

This work is dedicated to you. May you find solace in these pages and recognize your own strength reflected in them. You are not alone, and your experiences, though they may mark you, do not define the entirety of your being or your potential.

Let each word be a stepping stone from past to present, a tender guide from what was, to what can be. Here's to your renewal, your transformation, and the new harmonies you will create in the symphony of your life.

Table of Contents

Table of Contents

Welcome

Welcome to Harmony Mind Renewal

Dear Friend,

We are delighted to welcome you to Harmony Mind Renewal. As you embark on this ten-day endeavor, we aim to enrich your daily life with the practice of mindfulness, supported by a foundation of evidence-based research and time-honored wisdom.

Our program is built upon principles that are rooted in scientific inquiry and psychological understanding. We draw from the work of renowned experts such as Jon Kabat-Zinn, the founder of Mindfulness-Based Stress Reduction (MBSR), and the extensive research documented in "The Mindful Brain" by Dr. Daniel J. Siegel, which explore the transformative effects of mindfulness on the brain and overall well-being.

Each activity within Harmony Mind Renewal has been crafted with thoughtfulness, integrating insights from studies published in reputable journals such as "JAMA Internal Medicine" and "Psychosomatic Medicine," which have highlighted the positive impact of mindfulness meditation on mental health and stress reduction.

As a part of our community, you will join the Circle, a network of participants who are embarking on a similar path of self-discovery and support. Here, the art of mindfulness is not just practiced but also shared, creating a tapestry of collective experiences that enrich each individual's journey. Please approach this experience with an open mind, ready to explore the scientifically-backed practices that have been shown to foster resilience, enhance focus, and promote a greater sense of peace.

We look forward to guiding you through each step of this engaging and insightful experience.

The Role of Mindfulness in Personal Growth

In the bustling rhythm of modern life, the concept of personal growth often becomes overshadowed by the cacophony of daily responsibilities and digital distractions. Yet, it is within this very chaos that the serene practice of mindfulness emerges as a beacon of clarity and transformation.

At the heart of Harmony Mind Renewal, we embrace the role of mindfulness as a pivotal catalyst for personal growth. This journey is neither a race nor a solitary pursuit. It is a gentle unfolding, a deliberate attunement to the present moment that cultivates the soil of our inner landscape, allowing the seeds of our potential to sprout and flourish.

Scientific Roots in a Creative Odyssey
Mindfulness, a term that echoes through the corridors of both ancient traditions and contemporary psychology, is underpinned by a wealth of scientific evidence. Pioneers like Jon Kabat-Zinn have brought mindfulness into the therapeutic limelight, demonstrating that the mindful practice of simply being can powerfully recalibrate our stress responses and elevate our quality of life.

Neuroscientific research, including insights from Dr. Daniel J. Siegel's "The Mindful Brain," illustrates how mindfulness nurtures the very architecture of our brains. Through neuroplasticity, the deliberate focus on the here and now can rewire our neural pathways, enhancing emotional regulation, cognitive flexibility, and resilience against life's adversities.

A Warm Embrace of Growth
Within the nurturing embrace of Harmony Mind Renewal, mindfulness is more than a technique—it is an art form. Each breath becomes a brushstroke on the canvas of consciousness, each moment a note in the symphony of self-awareness. As you engage in our carefully curated practices, you will find yourself painting the portrait of your personal growth with each mindful act.

The Role of Mindfulness in Personal Growth

The Creative Synergy of Community

Beyond the self, the practice of mindfulness within the Circle offers a shared vibrancy, a collective heartbeat. Here, personal growth is amplified by the wisdom of the group, providing a chorus of support and inspiration. The Circle is not just a feature of our program—it is a crucible for the alchemy of transformation, where individual journeys converge and the power of community is harnessed.

Embarking on the Mindful Path

As you step forward into the embrace of Harmony Mind Renewal, remember: personal growth is an odyssey, not a sprint. It's a path paved with patience, presence, and a mindful approach to each day. With each step, you are not just moving; you are evolving, expanding, and embracing the full spectrum of what it means to grow.

Welcome to the first note of your symphony, the initial stroke of your masterpiece, the inaugural step on your path to personal growth through the art of mindfulness.

With open hearts and scientific minds, we journey together.

Harmony Mind Renewal beckons you to begin.

Day 1
Embracing Mindfulness

Day 1: Awakening Stillness within - Embracing Mindfulness

Welcome, fellow explorers, to a journey into the vast landscape of your inner world. Today, we begin with a foundational practice - the art of mindfulness meditation. This potent tool, honed over millennia, offers a sanctuary within the whirlwind of life, a portal to cultivate inner peace and radiant awareness.

10-Minute Mindfulness Meditation Oasis:
Prepare your sanctuary: Seek a haven, a quiet nook where you can settle for 10 minutes uninhibited. A comfy cushion, gentle light, and a trusty timer to mark your passage through stillness.

Step into quietude: Find a pose that feels just right, seated or lying down, allowing your spine to lengthen and your shoulders to soften. Close your eyes gently, or lower your gaze, inviting a sense of inwardness.

Breathe with awareness: With each inhalation, feel the cool air trace its path through your nostrils, down into your lungs, expanding your chest. Exhale slowly, releasing tension like leaves on a gentle breeze. Let your breath be your anchor, your guide in this serene voyage.

Observe the dance of thoughts: As you rest in the mindful embrace of your breath, thoughts and sensations may arise like passing clouds. Notice them without judgment, like observing the ever-changing sky. If your attention wanders, simply return your focus to the gentle rhythm of your breath, your steady anchor in the present moment.

Day 1
Embracing Mindfulness

Tips for your mindful journey:

- Embrace routine: Carving out a dedicated time each day for your practice strengthens its roots and nurtures its blossoming.
- Befriend distractions: Remember, wandering thoughts are natural guests in your inner landscape. Greet them with kindness, then gently guide your attention back to your breath.
- Find your comfort zone: Experiment with different postures to discover what allows you to settle deeply into your practice.
- Begin and end with gratitude: Bookend your meditation with a brief moment of appreciation for this time dedicated to your inner well-being.
- Openness is your compass: Approach this practice with curiosity and a gentle openness, allowing yourself to experience the quiet magic of the present moment.

Nourish your daily life with presence: As you step out of your mindful oasis, carry the stillness within. Each breath, a reminder to return to the sanctuary of your own being. Remember, science whispers wisdom of the brain's transformation through mindfulness - enhanced focus, a deeper understanding of self, and a haven from the storms of the external world. Let the simplicity of this practice be your guiding light, illuminating the path to inner peace and a life infused with mindful awareness.

With gentle encouragement and a shared belief in the transformative power of stillness, we embark on this journey together. Remember, you are not alone on this path of mindful exploration. May each day be a step closer to uncovering the treasures that lie within the depths of your being.

Parting Thoughts:
Let the echoes of your mindful journey resonate throughout your day. Remember, each moment is an opportunity to return to the quietude within, to reconnect with the gentle rhythm of your breath, and to experience the joy of simply being present.

Day 1
Embracing Mindfulness

Concluding the Session:
When the timer signals the end of your 10 minutes, slowly bring your awareness back to the room. Open your eyes if they were closed, and take a moment to notice how you feel.

Circle Reflection:
After concluding your meditation, spend one minute to check in with your Circle. Share a reflection or insight about your experience with today's meditation practice, listening to others as they do the same. This brief connection can deepen your practice and foster a shared sense of support within the group.

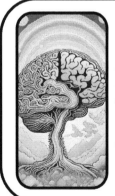

Take a moment to check in with your Circle and share your reflections about today's lesson. This is a valuable time to connect, reflect together, and support each other's journey.

Day 1
Reflection

Day 2
The Art of Grounding

Day 2: Inhabiting the Earth Within - Getting Grounded in Your Body

Welcome back, fellow explorers. Today, we turn inward, exploring the practice of body scan meditation. This simple yet powerful technique helps us connect with our own bodies, anchoring us in the present moment. It's like building a solid foundation for our mindfulness journey.

10-Minute Body Scan Expedition:
Find your haven: Seek a quiet corner where you can settle for 10 minutes without distractions. Sit or lie down in a comfortable position, with your spine long and shoulders relaxed. A timer can keep track of the time, but don't worry about it.

Anchor in now: Start with three deep breaths, feeling your body relax with each exhale. Let your breath be your guide, gently leading you inwards.

Exploring your landscape: Begin with your feet, those trusty anchors connecting you to the ground. Notice how they feel against the floor – warm, cool, flat, textured? Slowly move your awareness up your legs, feeling the pressure against your seat or the floor. Pay attention to your torso, the gentle rise and fall of your chest with each breath. Reach your fingertips, explore the map of your arms, then gently ascend to your neck and head. With each sensation, simply observe, without judgment. Just notice what's there.

Coming back together: Take one last deep breath, bringing your awareness back to your toes and fingers. Wiggle them playfully, reconnecting with your physical form. Gently open your eyes and take in your surroundings, feeling the wholeness of your body.

Day 2
The Art of Grounding

Navigating the Bodyscape:
Precision matters: As you explore, try to notice the tiny details of your sensations. Is your left foot warmer than your right? Are there different textures on your fingertips? This kind of attention deepens your connection to your body.

Acceptance is key: Be open to whatever you feel, even if it's uncomfortable. This practice isn't about changing your body, but simply learning its language.

Daily mapmaking: Consider making this body scan a daily ritual. The more you do it, the better you'll get at knowing your inner terrain, which makes you more mindful in every part of your life. Be patient: Don't get discouraged if it takes time to feel grounded. Just keep practicing, and celebrate even the small moments of awareness.

Mindful approach: Remember, this isn't about changing your body, but simply observing it. Be gentle with yourself, like a curious explorer discovering a new land.

Grounding for growth: Carry this sense of bodily awareness with you throughout your day. With each mindful breath, reconnect to the earth beneath your feet. Remember, your body isn't just a shell, but a vibrant source of information about yourself and the world around you.

Parting Thoughts:
Today, I celebrate the simple wisdom of my body. With each mindful scan, I deepen my roots in the present moment, feeling more grounded and peaceful. May this journey remind us that true strength and clarity come from connecting with our inner landscapes.
So, let's continue our mindful voyage together. Remember, you are not alone on this path. With each step, you're getting closer to discovering the inner strength and wisdom waiting within your own body.

I wish you a day filled with the simple joy of inhabiting your own being.

Day 2
The Art of Grounding

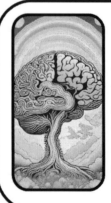 Take a moment now to connect with your Circle, offering your thoughts on today's topic. It's an enriching opportunity to engage, reflect as a collective, and provide support along your shared path.

Day 2
Reflection

Day 3
Gratitude as a Practice

Day 3: Blooming Gratitude - Growing Joy in Your Garden

Welcome back, travelers! Today, we explore the magical garden of gratitude, a practice that helps us see the good things in life and feel happier. Like planting seeds and watching them grow, when we appreciate things, we make our lives better and brighter.

10-Minute Gratitude Ritual:
Find your haven: Seek a quiet corner where you can sit or lie down for 10 minutes without interruptions. Make sure you're comfy, with your back straight and shoulders relaxed. Have a notebook or your phone ready to write down your thanks.

Planting Seeds of Thankfulness: Start with 3 deep breaths, letting go of any worries with each exhale. Now, think of something good that happened today, even if it's small. Maybe it was a delicious meal, a kind word from a friend, or the sunshine on your face. Write it down.
Harvesting Joy's Treasures: Now, list 2 more things you're grateful for. Think about the details – how did they make you feel? For example, instead of just writing "friend," write "My friend making me laugh until I cried." The more detail, the more joy you'll feel!

Blossoming in Your Mind: Close your eyes and imagine one of the things you wrote down. See it, feel it, and hear it – how does it make you happy? Let that happiness fill you up like sunshine.
Gratitude Rain Showers: Think back to your whole day. Did anyone do something nice for you? Did you have a fun experience? Take a moment to appreciate those things, even the small ones.

Day 3
Gratitude as a Practice

Tips for Growing Gratitude:

- Specifics make it sweeter: The more details you write down, the more you'll feel grateful. Instead of "food," write "the yummy pizza with extra cheese!"
- New seeds every day: Don't repeat the same things all the time. Look for new good things to be thankful for every day.
- Thorns can bloom too: Even bad things can teach us something or make us stronger. Be grateful for those lessons too!
- Share the sunshine: Tell your friends and family what you're grateful for. It makes everyone feel happier!
- Be gentle with yourself: Don't worry if you can't think of many things at first. Just keep practicing and you'll see more good things to be thankful for.

Keep Growing!

Do this gratitude ritual every day, like watering your garden. The more you do it, the more joy and happiness you'll grow in your life!

Parting Thoughts:

Carry the feeling of gratitude with you all day. Look for the good things, big and small, and appreciate them. Remember, you're not alone in this journey to happiness. We're all growing together, one thankful thought at a time.

May your gratitude bloom like a beautiful flower garden, and may your days be filled with sunshine and joy!

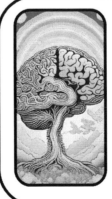

Pause to touch base with your Circle and exchange insights on today's teachings. Time is precious for fostering connection, collective contemplation, and bolstering one another's paths.

Day 3
Reflection

Day 4
Visualization for Inner Peace

Day 4: Paint Your Peace - Create Your Inner Calm Corner

Welcome back, fellow explorers! Today, we explore a powerful skill: using our imagination to build a peaceful haven within ourselves. Think of it as painting a picture in your mind, a place you can visit anytime to feel calm and relaxed.

Mind Magic:
Our brains are amazing! They can create worlds that aren't even real, and these imaginary places can affect our feelings. A scary picture can make us scared, but a peaceful one can help us feel calm. Today, we'll use this mind magic to build our own special calm corner.

10-Minute Peace Painting:
1. Find your cozy spot: Sit or lie down somewhere quiet for 10 minutes. Close your eyes or soften your gaze, letting your mind go inward. Take a few deep breaths, imagining you're releasing any worries or tension.
2. Meet your calm buddy: Think of someone or something who makes you feel peaceful. Maybe it's a wise mentor, a cuddly animal, or even just a feeling of quiet joy. Ask this "calm buddy" to guide you to your special haven.
3. Step through the shimmer: Imagine a glowing doorway, like a magical entrance to your inner world. Step through it with your calm buddy. This is your private haven, a place where you can feel totally safe and relaxed.
4. Use your senses: What does your haven look like? Is it a sunny beach, a cozy cabin, or a quiet garden? What do you see, hear, smell, and feel? Imagine the sand between your toes, the ocean waves whispering, or the flowers blooming. Let your senses fully experience the peace of your haven.
5. Carry the calm: Slowly open your eyes and take a breath. Hold onto the feeling of calm from your haven. It's like a warm blanket you can carry with you throughout your day. If you ever feel stressed, close your eyes and go back to your haven.

Day 4
Visualization for Inner Peace

Peace Tips:
- Paint it vivid: The more details you imagine, the better! Make your haven feel real and alive for you.
- Feel the good vibes: Let yourself enjoy the happiness, safety, and relaxation your haven brings.
- Daily visits: Come back to your haven every day, even for a few minutes. The more you visit, the stronger your inner peace becomes.
- Get creative: Your haven can be anything you want! Explore different places and see what brings you the most calm.
- Be kind to yourself: Don't worry if your pictures aren't perfect. Just relax and enjoy the process of creating your calm space.

Peace is Always with You:
Remember, the peace you feel in your haven is always with you. Whenever you feel stressed, take a moment to close your eyes and go back there. Breathe deeply, feel the calm, and let it wash over you. You have a superpower: the ability to create peace within yourself, and that's something to be proud of.

I wish you a day filled with the gentle glow of inner peace.

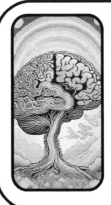

Give yourself a moment to sync with your Circle and express your thoughts on today's learning. It's a crucial time for nurturing connections, reflecting in unity, and aiding each other's journeys.

Day 4
Reflection

Day 5
Nurturing Self-Compassion
with Affirmations

Day 5: Growing Kindness Inside - Planting Words of Self-Love

Welcome back, fellow explorers! Today, we explore the beautiful garden of self-compassion, where we learn to be kind to ourselves like we would to a dear friend. By planting "seeds" of positive words, called affirmations, we can grow strong and happy, even when life gets tough.

Why Self-Compassion?
Imagine we all have delicate flowers inside us. Sometimes, we judge ourselves too harshly, like a harsh wind that can wilt our blooms. But with self-compassion, we become gentle gardeners, watering our flowers with kind words and making them grow tall and proud. Self-compassion helps us forgive ourselves for mistakes, believe in our worth, and face challenges with courage.

Planting Seeds of Love:
Affirmations are like magic seeds we plant in our minds. These positive phrases, when repeated like a whisper to ourselves, can blossom into strong feelings of confidence, resilience, and self-acceptance.

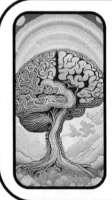

Dedicate a moment to engage with your Circle, discussing your thoughts on today's material. Cherish this opportunity to bond, deliberate as a group, and reinforce each other's progress.

Day 5
Nurturing Self-Compassion
with Affirmations

10-Minute Seed-Planting Exercise:

- Find your peaceful corner: Sit or lie down somewhere quiet for 10 minutes. Take a few deep breaths, letting go of worries and making space for kindness.

- Think of one area: Where would you like to be kinder to yourself? Maybe you struggle with accepting mistakes, believing in yourself, or dealing with difficult emotions. Choose one area to focus on today.
  - Plant your seeds: Now, craft a special saying for yourself, starting with "I am" or "I believe." Make it positive and true, like a sunny message to your flower. Here are some examples:For accepting mistakes: "I am human, and it's okay to make mistakes. I learn from them and grow stronger."
  - For believing in yourself: "I am capable and worthy of achieving my dreams. I trust my skills and my heart."
  - For dealing with difficult emotions: "I can handle hard feelings. They are like passing clouds, and I am the bright blue sky underneath."
  -

- Whisper with love: Choose 2-3 affirmations that feel most powerful to you. Repeat them silently or softly, with kindness and belief. Imagine these words sinking into your soil, taking root, and making your flowers bloom!

- Water your garden daily: Remember, self-compassion is like a beautiful garden. Keep planting your seeds (affirmations) every day, especially when you feel down. The more you care for your garden, the brighter and stronger it will grow!

Day 5
Nurturing Self-Compassion
with Affirmations

Tips for Growing Self-Love:

- Make it personal: The more your affirmations speak to your specific needs, the deeper they will grow in you.
- Positive and present: Use positive words and talk about yourself in the "now," like "I am strong" instead of "I will be strong."
- Be your own best friend: Speak to yourself with the same kindness and understanding you would offer a loved one.
- Keep practicing: Repeating affirmations takes time and patience. Be gentle with yourself and keep watering your garden!
- Enjoy the journey: Blooming from within is a beautiful process. Appreciate the progress you make and enjoy the feeling of becoming kinder to yourself.

Carry Kindness with You:
Let the seeds of self-compassion you planted today travel with you throughout your day. Remember your affirmations like gentle reminders of your worth and strength. You are unique and amazing, and deserve to bloom with confidence and joy!

Parting Thoughts:
As you leave your mindful haven, remember, you are not alone on this path of self-love. We are all learning to be kinder to ourselves, one step at a time. Trust the rhythm of your inner garden, nurture your seeds of compassion, and watch the beautiful flower of self-acceptance blossom within you.

With warm wishes for a day filled with the sunshine of self-compassion,

Day 5
Reflection

Day 6
Mastering the Art of Mindful Listening

Day 6: Listen Up! Become a Conversation Maestro in 10 Minutes

Welcome, fellow adventurers! Today, we're turning ourselves into superstars of listening – the kind who hear every note, understand the hidden beats, and make conversations sing! No more zoning out or waiting for our turn to talk. In just 10 minutes, we'll learn to listen like music conductors, weaving deeper connections and understanding into every conversation.

10-Minute Music Lesson:
1. Set the stage: Find a quiet, cozy spot with a friend or partner. Sit face-to-face, put away distractions, and take a few deep breaths together. This is your listening zone – a stage for words to flow like a beautiful melody.
2. Be a detective: As your friend speaks, become a super-sleuth. Don't just hear the words, but listen to the whole song: the rhythm of their voice, the twinkle in their eyes, maybe even the way they shift in their chair. Notice these tiny clues that tell you the real story behind their words.
3. Put on their shoes: Imagine stepping into your friend's shoes for a moment. What might be going on in their world? What feelings are they playing? It's not about agreeing with everything, but about understanding their unique tune.
4. Echo the melody: Gently reflect what you hear. A simple "I understand you're saying..." or "It sounds like you're feeling..." can work wonders. You're not repeating, you're showing you're paying attention and inviting them to play a bit more.
5. The magic of silence: Don't rush to fill the space between notes. Let the quiet work its magic. Silence gives your friend time to think, feel heard, and maybe even surprise you with a deeper song.

Day 6
Mastering the Art of Mindful Listening

Daily Listening Tips:

- Let the music flow: Relax and let the conversation unfold naturally. Don't force things or jump to conclusions – just enjoy the rhythm.
- Celebrate baby steps: Remember, becoming a listening master takes time. Be proud of every step you take, even if it's just noticing a few extra "tells" today.
- Expand your orchestra: Play this listening game with everyone – friends, family, even strangers at the bus stop. You'll be amazed at the connections you build!

Carry the Music with You:

As you step back into the world, take the melody of deep listening with you. Let your eyes see beyond words, your heart feel emotions unspoken, and your presence be a gift to those you meet. Remember, the world is a beautiful symphony waiting to be heard. By becoming a mindful listener, you become not just a participant, but a conductor, weaving harmonies of understanding and connection everywhere you go.

With open ears and warm hearts, we continue our journey of human connection together. You are not alone on this path to deeper understanding. May each day be filled with the rich music of mindful listening.

Now, go out there and make some beautiful conversation music!

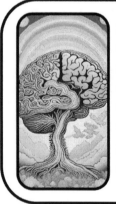

Dedicate a moment to engage with your Circle, discussing your thoughts on today's material. Cherish this opportunity to bond, deliberate as a group, and reinforce each other's progress.

Day 6
Reflection

Day 7
Circle of Growth

Day 7: Building Mindful Relationships with the Circle of Growth Worksheet

Today, as we embark on Day 7, we turn our attention to the intricate web of relationships that enrich our lives. By using the Circle of Growth Worksheet, we will engage in a meaningful exercise to map out and assess the state of our interpersonal connections. This reflective practice will help us bring mindfulness into how we relate to those who share our journey.

Instructions:
Preparation: Have the Circle of Growth Worksheet ready in front of you. Ensure you're in a quiet space where you can contemplate undisturbed.

Quieting the Mind: Take a few deep breaths to center yourself. Ground your thoughts in the present and prepare to engage with the worksheet with honesty and openness.

Listing Relationships: Begin by listing 27 people who play a role in your life. These could be family members, friends, colleagues, or acquaintances. Simply write their names down in the space provided.

Defining Roles: Next to each name, note the role they play in your life. For example, 'mentor,' 'partner,' 'friend,' 'colleague,' etc. This will help contextualize your relationship with each person.

Rating Your Relationships: Assign a rating of Flourishing, Budding, or Dormant to each person based on the current state of your relationship with them:
- Flourishing: Represents strong, healthy relationships that are a priority in your life.
- Budding: Indicates relationships that are important but may need more attention or have room for improvement.
- Dormant: Denotes relationships that are challenging, distant, or perhaps need reevaluation.

Day 7
Circle of Growth

Reflective Analysis: Spend the remaining time contemplating why you've assigned these ratings. Consider what actions might improve a Budding relationship to a Flourishing, or how you might address the challenges within a Dormant relationship.

Commitment to Growth: Choose one relationship you've rated as Budding or Dormant, a connection holding potential yet in need of attention. Consider two paths of growth:

Nurturing the Connection:
- Initiate a conversation: Reach out and share something heartfelt, ask a question, or propose an activity to rekindle the bond.
- Express gratitude: Recognize the value this person brings, perhaps through a written note, a sincere appreciation, or a gesture of kindness.
- Offer a listening ear: Dedicate quality time to truly hear their thoughts and feelings, creating a safe space for open communication.
- Extend forgiveness: Let go of past hurts, offering understanding and a fresh start to the relationship.

Identifying Boundaries:
- Set clear expectations: Communicate your needs and preferences regarding communication, interaction, and support within the relationship.
- Limit your availability: Establish healthy boundaries around your time and energy, ensuring you prioritize your own well-being.
- Choose communication channels: Decide on suitable ways to interact, perhaps setting limits on specific channels or topics to protect your emotional space.
- Seek external support: Consider talking to a trusted friend, family member, or therapist to gain perspective and develop healthy coping mechanisms for navigating this relationship.

Day 7
Circle of Growth

Reflective Analysis: Spend the remaining time contemplating why you've assigned these ratings. Consider what actions might improve a Budding relationship to a Flourishing, or how you might address the challenges within a Dormant relationship.

Commitment to Growth: Choose one relationship you've rated as Budding or Dormant, a connection holding potential yet in need of attention. Consider two paths of growth:

Nurturing the Connection:
- Initiate a conversation: Reach out and share something heartfelt, ask a question, or propose an activity to rekindle the bond.
- Express gratitude: Recognize the value this person brings, perhaps through a written note, a sincere appreciation, or a gesture of kindness.
- Offer a listening ear: Dedicate quality time to truly hear their thoughts and feelings, creating a safe space for open communication.
- Extend forgiveness: Let go of past hurts, offering understanding and a fresh start to the relationship.

Identifying Boundaries:
- Set clear expectations: Communicate your needs and preferences regarding communication, interaction, and support within the relationship.
- Limit your availability: Establish healthy boundaries around your time and energy, ensuring you prioritize your own well-being.
- Choose communication channels: Decide on suitable ways to interact, perhaps setting limits on specific channels or topics to protect your emotional space.
- Seek external support: Consider talking to a trusted friend, family member, or therapist to gain perspective and develop healthy coping mechanisms for navigating this relationship.

Day 7
Circle of Growth

Remember, choosing one path doesn't preclude the other. As you nurture the connection, identifying healthy boundaries can foster mutual respect and strengthen your well-being within the relationship.

Ultimately, the choice is yours. Listen to your intuition, and trust your understanding of what will serve you and the relationship best. With mindful action and open communication, you can pave the way for stronger bonds and greater harmony in your connections.

Closing Reflection: After completing the activity, close your eyes for a brief moment. Acknowledge the value each person brings to your life and the role you play in theirs.

Tips for Today:
- Honesty is Crucial: Be truthful in your assessment for this exercise to be meaningful.
- Privacy Matters: Your ratings are for your personal use and reflection. They are not to be shared but to guide you in strengthening your relationships.
- Mindful Approach: Remember, this is not about judgment but about awareness and growth.
- Continued Practice: Consider revisiting this worksheet every month to reflect on how your relationships have evolved and what new actions you might take.

Parting Thoughts:
Day 7's activity serves as a powerful reminder of the interconnectedness of our lives. By mindfully assessing and categorizing the state of our relationships, we gain clarity on where our emotional investments lie and where we might need to redirect our efforts. Carry forward the intentionality cultivated today into your daily interactions, and observe the positive transformations that ensue in the tapestry of your relationships.

Today, I embrace the power of my relationships, committing to nurture them with kindness, understanding, and the mindful presence that fosters true connection.

CIRCLE OF GROWTH

NAME	ROLE	RATING

Day 7
Reflection

Day 8
Nature's Embrace

Day 8: Nature's Embrace - Finding Peace Indoors or Out

Welcome back, fellow explorers! Today, we delve into the comforting embrace of nature, whether we seek it under rustling leaves or within the cozy walls of our home. The great outdoors isn't our only portal to peace – nature holds its magic even when the skies weep. Let's discover how to connect with this calming energy wherever we may find ourselves.

Green Adventures from Anywhere:

Outdoor Nature Walk: (If skies permit)

- Forest Bathing: Immerse yourself in a nearby park or forest. Breathe deeply, letting the scent of trees and earth fill your lungs. Notice the sunlight filtering through branches, the vibrant dance of leaves, the melody of birdsong. Feel the ground beneath your feet, grounding yourself in the present moment.

- Barefoot Bliss: Find a grassy patch, shed your shoes, and connect with the earth directly. Savor the coolness or warmth, the tickle of blades on your skin. This simple act can release tension and ground you in the present.

- Sensory Feast: Engage all your senses. Listen to the wind in the trees, the chirping of birds, the rustle of leaves. Close your eyes and smell the damp earth, pine needles, or blooming flowers. Touch the rough bark of a tree, the smooth curve of a pebble. Immerse yourself in the symphony of nature.

Day 8
Nature's Embrace

Indoor Nature Haven: (For rainy days)

- Window Walk: Turn your window into a portal to the green world. Observe the leaves swaying in the wind, birds flitting by, or clouds drifting across the sky. Breathe deeply, imagining the fresh air filling your lungs, and let the scene soothe your mind.

- Green Book Escape: Dive into a nature-themed book or travel documentary. Lose yourself in captivating landscapes, fascinating wildlife, or the adventures of fellow nature lovers. Let the words and images transport you to a peaceful green haven.

- Herb Garden Symphony: Create a mini herb garden on your windowsill. Tend to it daily, noticing the delicate fragrance of basil, the vibrant green of mint, the gentle touch of sprouting seeds. This nurturing act can promote calm and reduce stress.

- Nature Soundscape: Create a calming playlist of nature sounds – flowing water, rustling leaves, bird calls, or ocean waves. Listen with headphones or softly in the background, letting the sounds wash away worries and lull you into a peaceful state.

Carry Nature's Peace:

No matter where you find yourself, hold onto the calming essence of nature. Close your eyes and recall a peaceful moment, indoors or out. Breathe deeply and feel the tension melt away. Remember, nature's peace is always within reach, waiting to be embraced.

Day 8 Tips:

- Start small: Even a few minutes of mindful connection can make a difference.
- Find your green space: Whether it's a park, your backyard, or a window, create a space for connecting with nature.
- Be present: Put away distractions and immerse yourself fully in the experience.
- Make it a habit: Dedicate time each day to connect with nature, even in small ways.
- Share the joy: Invite friends or family to join you on your nature adventures, both indoors and out.

Day 8
Nature's Embrace

With open hearts and open minds, let's welcome the embrace of nature, in its infinite forms, and discover the endless wellspring of calm it offers.

May your day be filled with the gentle melody of inner peace, wherever you find it.

Your Fellow Traveler on the Path to Inner Sanctuary

This revised version offers both outdoor and indoor activities, making it accessible to everyone regardless of weather conditions. The language remains simple and direct, and the focus is on practical steps for connecting with nature and finding inner peace. I hope this is what you were looking for!

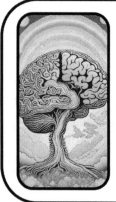

Dedicate a moment to engage with your Circle, discussing your thoughts on today's material. Cherish this opportunity to bond, deliberate as a group, and reinforce each other's progress.

Day 8
Reflection

Day 9
The Power of Expressive Writing

Day 9: Words Like Wild Horses - Unleash Your Creativity!

Welcome, fellow story weavers! Today, we explore a fun way to play with words, called "wild writing." It's like letting your thoughts run free, like a herd of horses galloping across a field! No rules, no judges, just you and your pen, painting pictures with words.

What is Wild Writing?

Imagine your mind is a treasure chest overflowing with ideas, feelings, and stories. Wild writing is like opening that chest and letting everything tumble out, all at once, just like it is! It's about not worrying if things make sense or follow a perfect path. It's about letting your words run wild, like horses in a meadow, and seeing where they take you.

Why Go Wild?

This free-flowing writing can be a magic trick for your brain:
- Unleash the Story Horses: It helps your imagination run wild, like a playful foal, and come up with new ideas for stories, poems, or even just silly jokes.
- Get to Know Yourself: By letting your thoughts run free, you learn more about what's inside you, like hidden feelings or secret dreams.
- Calm the Stormy Clouds: Sometimes, when we write freely, our worries and anxieties can spill out onto the page, like rain clouds clearing the sky. This can make us feel lighter and happier!
- Focus on Now: Wild writing helps us stay in the present moment, like a bird watching the world go by. We just write what's in our minds, right now, without worrying about the future or the past.

Day 9
The Power of Expressive Writing

Ready to Saddle Up?

Here's your trusty steed for this adventure:

- Find your quiet corner: Choose a cozy spot where you won't be interrupted. Grab a pen and paper, or your favorite writing tool – whatever makes your creative horses neigh with excitement!
- Take a deep breath: Let go of any worries or doubts. Imagine you're a painter, ready to splash colors onto a blank canvas.
- Let the words gallop: Start writing whatever pops into your head, big or small, silly or serious. Don't worry about grammar, spelling, or even making sense! Just let your words flow like a river, one sentence after another.
- Follow the trail: If you get stuck, don't worry! Just write something like "stuck" or "lost," and see where your thoughts take you next. Remember, your wild horses might change direction suddenly, and that's okay!
- Enjoy the ride: Don't judge your writing or be afraid of what you uncover. This is just for you, a chance to explore your own world of words.
- Pat your horse: When time is up, take a moment to look at what you wrote. You might be surprised by the hidden gems you find – a funny phrase, a spark of a story, or even just a new way of seeing yourself.

More Ways to Play with Words:

- Word Whispers: Give yourself a starting word, like "banana" or "dream," and see where it leads you.
- Timed Races: Set a timer for 5 minutes and write as fast as you can, like a wild horse racing through a field!
- Story Swap: Write with a friend or family member, taking turns adding sentences to the same story. See how your wild horses can create something amazing together!

Day 9
The Power of Expressive Writing

Remember: Wild writing is all about having fun and exploring your creativity. There are no right or wrong answers, just the joy of letting your words run free. So, grab your pen, hop on your trusty steed, and let your imagination gallop into the wild world of words!

Day 9 Tips:

- Be kind to yourself: This is a safe space for your words to play. No one will judge you, so relax and have fun!
- Experiment and play: Try different prompts, tools, and ways of writing. See what makes your creative horses neigh with excitement!
- Write often: The more you practice, the easier it gets to let your words run wild.
- Share your adventures: If you feel comfortable, share your wild writing with a friend or writing group. They might be inspired by your journey!

With open hearts and playful spirits, let's unleash our inner wordsmiths and see what creative treasures we discover on this wild writing adventure!

May your Day 9 be filled with the magic of your own unique voice!

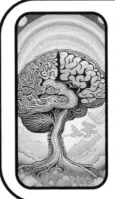

Dedicate a moment to engage with your Circle, discussing your thoughts on today's material. Cherish this opportunity to bond, deliberate as a group, and reinforce each other's progress.

Day 9
Reflection

Day 10
Celebrate

Day 10: A Toast to You, Mindful Explorer!

Well, here we stand, ten sunrises and ten moonlit walks later, on the peak of our mindful mountain trail. Congratulations, fellow adventurer! You've scaled the hills of self-awareness, navigated the valleys of introspection, and emerged with a brighter smile and a lighter heart.

Look how far you've come:
- You've woven mindfulness into the tapestry of your days, breathing deeply even in the whirlwind.
- You've nurtured your relationships with gentle care, building bridges of understanding and affection.
- You've embraced nature's calming embrace, finding peace in rustling leaves and sun-dappled meadows.
- You've unleashed your creativity, letting words flow like a wild river, painting pictures with your pen.

This journey wasn't just about ticking boxes or reaching goals. It was about planting seeds of mindfulness within you, seeds that will continue to sprout and blossom with each passing day.

Now, the question arises: where does the path lead next?

Day 10
Celebrate

Planning for Your Mindful Future:

We understand that every mountain climber eventually reaches the base, ready for new peaks. So, before we bid farewell, let's explore the possibilities:

- Continue the Adventure: Join us for further mindful explorations! We have exciting journeys planned, delving deeper into themes like inner peace, mindful communication, and cultivating joy.
- Chart Your Own Course: Take the tools and learnings from these ten days and forge your own mindful path. We'll always be here as your companion, cheering you on as you explore the vast landscape of inner awareness.
- Rest and Integrate: Sometimes, the best way forward is to simply pause and let the experiences of the past ten days settle within you. Allow the seeds of mindfulness to take root, silently shaping your thoughts and actions.

No matter which path you choose, remember one thing: the mindful spirit you've awakened within you is yours to keep. Carry it with you as you navigate the joys and challenges of life, and watch it transform your world, one mindful moment at a time.

Before we step off the mountaintop, please share your thoughts with us through a quick survey:

- How much did you enjoy the past ten days of mindful exploration? (Highly enjoyable, Somewhat enjoyable, Not very enjoyable)
- Would you be interested in joining us for further mindful adventures? (Yes, Definitely, Maybe not, Not at this time)
- Did you find the activities and exercises helpful in your journey towards mindfulness? (Very helpful, Somewhat helpful, Not very helpful)
- Is there anything you would like to see included in future mindful programs? (Please share your thoughts!)

Day 10
Celebrate

Your feedback is precious to us as we continue to guide others on the path to inner peace and well-being. Thank you for joining us on this journey, and remember, the mindful adventure never truly ends. Keep breathing, keep exploring, and keep shining your light.

Onward to a mindful future,

Your Fellow Traveler on the Path to Inner Sanctuary

Day 10
Reflection

In Proud Recognition

of

Completion of Harmony Mind Renewal

Through ten days of mindful practices and insightful reflections, you've cultivated a deeper understanding of yourself and the world around you.

This certificate acknowledges your:

Open Heart: For allowing yourself to explore the depths of your emotions and connect with compassion.

Curious Mind: For asking questions, seeking answers, and embracing the journey of self-discovery.

Present Moment: For finding tranquility in the present, untethered from past worries and future anxieties.

Creative Spark: For igniting your unique expression, letting your voice be heard, and sharing your light with the world.

May this certificate remind you to continue nurturing these qualities as you step forward on your path to well-being and joy.

Name

Date

RQLRN

Even More Mindfulness Practices

Grounding Walk Outside

Embrace the serenity of nature with a mindful walk. Let the simplicity of each step ground you in the present moment, as you breathe in harmony with the natural world around you.

Body Scan Meditation

Engage in a journey through your body, acknowledging each area with kindness. This meditation nurtures a deep state of relaxation, promoting inner tranquility and renewal.

Flower Meditation

Immerse yourself in the delicate details of a flower. This meditation enhances your focus on the present, inviting a sense of calm as you connect with the bloom's intricate beauty.

Movement Meditation

Let the rhythm guide you into a state of flow. As you move with intention, celebrate the freedom of expression and the joy of being present in your body.

Cleansing with Your Favorite Incense

Surround yourself with the purifying scent of incense. This practice aids in releasing stagnant energy and cultivating a space of clarity and focus.

Even More Mindfulness Practices

Tea Meditation 🍵

Sip your way to serenity. The simple act of drinking tea mindfully can be a soothing ritual, fostering peace and presence with every taste.

Nature Sound Meditation 🌿

Tune into the orchestra of nature. The symphony of natural sounds can help you find a deep sense of peace and connection to the world around you.

Visualize Healing White Light 🧘

Envision a radiant white light enveloping you, its purity healing and refreshing your spirit. This visualization can be a powerful tool for cleansing the mind and body.

Stretch Each Muscle Group 💪

Gently awaken your body with mindful stretching. As you release physical tension, you also let go of mental stress, creating harmony between body and mind.

Reflective Walking 🚶

Wander with purpose, reflecting on life's journey. This contemplative walk can offer insights and clarity, grounding you in mindfulness.

Restorative Yoga 🧘

Embrace the stillness of restorative yoga poses. In these moments of gentle stretch and reflection, find a deep sense of relaxation and balance.armony. This centered breathing calms the mind and aligns your energy.

Even More Mindfulness Practices

Gratitude Journaling

Cultivate an attitude of gratitude. Reflecting on the positives in your life can shift your mindset and open your heart to joy.

Creative Writing

Channel your inner muse through the art of writing. This form of self-expression can be a creative outlet for emotions, thoughts, and dreams.

Mindful Eating

Transform each meal into a mindful experience. Savor the flavors, textures, and nourishment your food provides, creating a deeper connection with your eating habits.

Guided Visualization Meditation

Embark on a mental voyage with guided imagery. These narratives can lead you to hidden inner sanctuaries of peace and inspiration.

Five Senses Exercise

Engage all your senses in a celebration of the present moment. This full-sensory experience can anchor you in the now and enhance your awareness.

Mindful Digital Detox

Unplug to recharge your mind. A break from digital noise can be a gateway to deeper self-connection and mindfulness.

Harmonizing Breath

Discover the power of your breath as a tool for harmony. This centered breathing calms the mind and aligns your energy.

Even More Mindfulness Practices

Mindful Reflection ✍
End your day with introspection. Reflecting on your experiences can foster growth and a peaceful state of mind.

Progressive Muscle Relaxation 🦵
Release the day's tension with a systematic relaxation of each muscle group. This practice promotes a restful state of being, preparing you for rejuvenation.

Mindful Digital Photography 📷
Capture the world through a mindful lens. This practice encourages you to see the extraordinary in the ordinary, deepening your appreciation for life's details.

Self-Massage 💆
Nurture your body with the healing touch of self-massage. This act of self-care can relieve tension and cultivate a loving connection with yourself.

Visualization with Nature 🏝
Retreat into a natural sanctuary within your mind. This visualization can be a restorative escape, filling you with a sense of peace and wonder.

Mindful Listening 🎶
Listen with intent to the sounds that surround you. This practice can deepen your connection to your environment and the present moment.

Laughter Yoga 🤸
Embrace the joy of laughter with laughter yoga. This unique practice combines laughter exercises with yogic breathing, promoting joy, stress relief, and an overall sense of well-being.

Even More Mindfulness Practices

Art Therapy 🎨
Delve into the world of colors and shapes with art therapy. Expressing yourself through art can help process emotions and foster mindfulness.

Mindful Coloring ✏️
Reconnect with the simplicity of childhood through mindful coloring. This soothing activity can help reduce stress and bring your focus to the present.

Forest Bathing (Shinrin-Yoku) 🌲
Immerse yourself in the healing atmosphere of a forest with Shinrin-Yoku. This Japanese practice encourages absorption of the forest atmosphere for therapeutic effects.

Aromatherapy 🌿
Engage your sense of smell with aromatherapy. The essential oils used can have various benefits, including relaxation and improved mood.

Gazing Meditation (Trataka) 👁️
Focus your gaze on an external object, such as a candle flame, to practice Trataka. This form of meditation can improve concentration and mental clarity.

Balloon Breathing Exercise 🎈
Visualize filling a balloon as you inhale deeply, expanding your lungs and belly, and slowly releasing the air as you exhale, deflating the imaginary balloon. This helps in regulating breath and calming the mind.

Sand Tray Therapy 🏖️
Arrange figures and shapes in a tray of sand to represent feelings and experiences. This tactile activity encourages expression and reflection.

Even More Mindfulness Practices

Mindful Bead Stringing 🔍
String beads mindfully, focusing on the color, texture, and pattern. This can be a meditative and calming activity that also improves fine motor skills.

Nature Crafting 🍂
Create art from natural elements like leaves, twigs, and stones. Engage with the materials mindfully, appreciating their unique qualities.

Palming for Eyes Relaxation 🙌
Rub your hands together to create warmth and then gently cup your palms over your closed eyes. The darkness and warmth can be soothing and restorative.

Mindful Humming 🎶
Hum a tune and feel the vibrations in your body. This simple activity can be soothing and help focus the mind.

Guided Self-Compassion Break 🖤
Take a moment to speak kindly to yourself, acknowledging your struggles and offering words of support and love, as you would to a friend.

Conscious Coloring with Mandalas 🌀
Color mandalas with intention and focus. The repetitive patterns can be a form of active meditation and relaxation.

Mindful Collage Creation ✂️
Create a collage from magazines or printed images. Focus on the process of selecting and arranging the images to express your thoughts and feelings.

Even More Mindfulness Practices

Tactile Sensation Box 🪨
Fill a box with various textured items and explore each one with your hands, noting the sensations and your emotional reactions to them.

Guided Imagery Journey 🖼️
Take a guided mental journey through a peaceful landscape, using vivid imagery to engage the senses and promote relaxation.

Mindful Observation of Art 🖼️
Spend time observing a piece of art, noticing the colors, shapes, and feelings it evokes without judgment.

Heartbeat Exercise 💜
Place your hand on your heart and feel your heartbeat. Sync your breath with your heartbeat to cultivate inner calm and presence.

Cloud Shaping ☁️
Lie down and watch the clouds, imagining them forming into shapes. This practice encourages creativity and a light-hearted approach to mindfulness.

Mindful Rock Balancing 🪨
Balance rocks on top of one another, which requires patience, concentration, and a gentle touch, fostering a meditative state of mind.

Aroma Dough Kneading 🍞
Create your own scented dough using flour, water, salt, and essential oils. As you knead the dough, focus on the texture and the scent. The act of kneading can be therapeutic, and the aroma adds a sensory dimension that can enhance the mindfulness experience.

Closing Thoughts

Closing Thoughts: Encouraging Ongoing Practice

As we draw the curtains on this chapter of our journey at Harmony Mind Renewal, we reflect on the experiences that have shaped our understanding and the bonds that have strengthened our resolve. The practice of mindfulness is not confined to the time we've spent together; it is a continuous odyssey that extends into the tapestry of our everyday lives.

The Seed of Mindfulness

Imagine the mindfulness you've cultivated as a seed planted in the fertile soil of your consciousness. With each day's practice, you've watered and nurtured this seed. As you move forward, it is vital to continue this care, allowing the roots of awareness to delve deeper, and the shoots of presence to reach higher.

The Rhythm of Daily Renewal

Incorporate the essence of mindfulness into the rhythm of your daily routine. Let it be as natural as breathing, as deliberate as the steps you take, and as consistent as the sunrise. It could manifest in a morning meditation, a mindful walk, or simply being fully present as you listen to a friend.

The Circle of Continuity

Your Circle — a tapestry of supportive peers — remains with you beyond our structured sessions. Lean on this community, share your milestones, and seek inspiration from the collective wisdom that pulses within it. The Circle is a reminder that while the practice is personal, the journey is shared.

Tools for the Path Ahead

The Circle of Growth Worksheet and other tools you've encountered are yours to revisit and refine. Use them as compasses to navigate through life's ebbs and flows, and as mirrors to reflect on your growth.

Closing Thoughts

Lifelong Learning
Embrace the concept of lifelong learning. Mindfulness is an evolving practice, one that adapts and grows with you. Seek out new knowledge, explore different techniques, and be open to the lessons that life presents.

The Infinite Cycle of Growth
Remember, personal growth is an infinite cycle. With each mindful moment, you are both the teacher and the student, the sculptor and the clay. You have the power to shape your experiences and, in turn, be shaped by them.

Final Affirmation
As we part ways, affirm to yourself:
I am a vessel of mindfulness,
Within me lies the serenity of the present,
The wisdom of the past,
And the seeds of tomorrow's growth.

Carry this affirmation with you as a beacon of Harmony Mind Renewal's enduring spirit.
In gratitude and with heartfelt wishes for your continued journey, we bid you peace, presence, and perpetual growth.

Lots of love to you,

Raquel René Martin
Harmony Mind Renewal
RQLRN
harmony@rqlrn.com
(928) 374-0011

Mindfulness Meditation Scripts

Appendix: Simple Mindfulness Meditation Scripts

1. Body Scan for Beginners:

- Find a comfortable sitting or lying position, eyes closed or softly focused.
- Take a few deep breaths, feeling your chest and belly rise and fall.
- Bring your attention to your toes, noticing any sensations like warmth, tingling, or pressure.
- Slowly scan your body upwards, paying attention to each part without judgment: ankles, calves, knees, thighs, hips.
- Continue to your abdomen, chest, shoulders, neck, and head. Observe any tension or tightness, releasing it with a gentle exhale.
- Reach the crown of your head and imagine a soft white light radiating from within you, spreading peace throughout your body.
- Take a few final deep breaths, feeling calm and grounded. Slowly open your eyes, carrying this sense of peace into your day.

2. Gratitude Meditation:

- Sit or lie comfortably, closing your eyes or allowing your gaze to soften.
- Recall a simple thing you're grateful for in the present moment. It could be anything, from the warmth of the sun on your skin to the taste of your morning coffee.
- Imagine holding this gratitude like a precious object in your hands, feeling its weight and significance.
- Let this feeling of gratitude expand, radiating outwards to encompass other things you're grateful for today, big or small.
- Allow yourself to bask in this warmth of appreciation, savoring each moment.
- When you're ready, gently release the feelings and open your eyes, carrying the glow of gratitude into your interactions and activities.

Mindfulness Meditation Scripts

3. Nature Mindfulness Walk:
- Find a peaceful outdoor space, a park, garden, or even your own backyard.
- Take a few deep breaths, connecting with the fresh air and natural sounds.
- Notice the details around you: the texture of leaves, the sway of branches, the chirping of birds.
- Walk slowly and deliberately, focusing on the sensation of your feet touching the ground.
- Engage all your senses: smell the flowers, feel the breeze on your skin, listen to the rustling leaves.
- Breathe deeply, imagining the clean air purifying your body and mind.
- If your mind wanders, gently bring your attention back to the present moment, to the sights, sounds, and sensations of nature.
- Spend as much time as you wish enjoying this mindful walk, allowing yourself to recharge in the embrace of nature.

These simple scripts offer a variety of options for beginners and seasoned practitioners alike.

Remember, the most important aspect is to relax, be present, and enjoy the journey of your own mindful experience.

Additional Resources

Books:

- "Your Brain on Art: How the Arts Transform Us" by Susan Magsamen and Ivy Ross is a groundbreaking exploration into the field of neuroaesthetics, revealing the transformative power of the arts on our brains and bodies. The book, a New York Times bestseller and recognized by Bloomberg as one of the best books of the year, takes readers on an evidence-backed journey, showing how participation in the arts can significantly improve health, promote individual flourishing, and foster stronger community ties.Through engaging research and expert conversations, including insights from figures like David Byrne and E. O. Wilson, the authors demonstrate how even brief art encounters can reduce stress, extend lifespans, and boost cognitive function. With its persuasive argument that the arts are not a mere luxury but a necessity for well-being, "Your Brain on Art" is a compelling guide, offering fresh perspectives on how the arts can reshape conventional medicine, create healthier communities, and heal our planet.

- Erika Buenaflor, M.A., J.D., is an author known for her work on curanderismo, which is a traditional healing practice in Mesoamerican culture, rather than mainstream mindfulness as it is commonly understood in the context of meditation and stress reduction. Her books typically revolve around ancient healing practices, rituals, and spiritual cleansings derived from her study and practice as a curandera.If you are interested in a mindfulness-related approach within the context of Mesoamerican spirituality, you might explore her book:"Cleansing Rites of Curanderismo: Limpias Espirituales of Ancient Mesoamerican Shamans" In this book, while the primary focus is on traditional healing rituals, there may be elements that overlap with the concept of mindfulness, such as being present in the moment, connecting with the self, and using ritual to foster a meditative state.

- "Project UnLonely: Healing Our Crisis of Disconnection" by Jeremy Nobel MD confronts the deepening loneliness epidemic. Nobel, who initiated Project UnLonely, explores loneliness in its many forms, from stark isolation to the distress of feeling out of place. He brings perspectives from various experts and those affected by loneliness, highlighting the pandemic's role in deepening not only physical but emotional disconnection. Nobel spotlights creativity as a remedy for loneliness, promoting it as a universal key to forge and maintain connections. "Project UnLonely" advocates for creative engagement as a powerful catalyst for reconnection with ourselves and others, offering hope and practical strategies for a society seeking to heal from disconnection.

FAQ

Frequently Asked Questions (FAQs) for Harmony Mind Renewal

Welcome to the FAQ section for Harmony Mind Renewal, where we offer a dedicated space for individuals with childhood trauma and those seeking to cultivate their mindfulness practices. Here are answers to some of the most common questions about our program.

What is Harmony Mind Renewal?

Harmony Mind Renewal is a 10-day, peer-led, online mindfulness group that provides a supportive community for those who have experienced childhood trauma and for anyone who wishes to improve their mindfulness practices.

Who should join Harmony Mind Renewal?

Our program is designed for individuals who have experienced childhood trauma and for those who are looking to deepen their mindfulness practice in a supportive community setting.
How is the program structured?

Participants in the program are expected to check in daily by posting a 1-minute video on the Marco Polo app. Additionally, you are encouraged to spend at least another minute each day responding to other participants' videos, offering feedback and support.

How do I sign up for Harmony Mind Renewal?
To sign up, please text your Adverse Childhood Experiences (ACEs) quiz score to Raquel René Martin at 928-374-0011, either via phone text or WhatsApp or email harmony@rqlrn.com.

What if I miss a day or fall behind in the program?
While all members are expected to check in daily for the duration of the 10-day program, we understand that life happens, and we offer grace when you need it. The important part is to stay engaged and connected with the group as much as possible.

Is there a cost for joining the program or using the Marco Polo app?
No, both the Harmony Mind Renewal program and the Marco Polo app are free to use.

FAQ

What can participants expect to gain from the 10-day experience?

Participants can expect to develop mindfulness skills, feel supported in a community of peers, and learn strategies to manage the ongoing effects of childhood trauma. The program also aims to promote personal growth and healing.

Do I need any experience with mindfulness to join?
No previous mindfulness experience is necessary. Our program is inclusive and designed to be beneficial for both beginners and those with more mindfulness practice.

How much time will the program require each day?
The program involves a daily commitment of 10 minutes to complete the day's exercise, a 1-minute check-in video and to spend at least another minute engaging with fellow participants, making it a manageable addition to most daily routines.

Can we stay connected with the group after the 10 days are over?
Harmony Mind Renewal is an ongoing program, you are welcome to join us for days 11 to 100 and beyond, participants often form lasting connections and may choose to continue supporting each as lifelong friends.

Who do I contact if I have any questions or issues with the program?
For any inquiries or support related to the Harmony Mind Renewal program, you can email our team at harmony@rqlrn.com.

Thank you for your interest in Harmony Mind Renewal. We're dedicated to providing a nurturing environment for healing and growth through mindfulness, and we look forward to having you join our community.

About the Creator

Raquel: Bridging Science, Spirit, and Healing in a Mindful Tapestry

Welcome to a space where vulnerability becomes strength, and healing embraces every thread of your journey. I'm Raquel, not just a CEO, mother, and grandmother, but a fellow traveler on the path towards a calmer, more vibrant life.

My story is woven with both hardship and grace. At 16, I faced the precipice of death from bacterial meningitis. Yet, a profound connection to my spiritual ancestor granted me a second chance.

Life wasn't solely defined by this extraordinary moment. My twenties saw me delve into ancestral medicine through body piercing, leading to successful studios and contributions to the Association of Professional Piercers. My thirties ushered in a publishing adventure, navigating the world of art, music, and culture. And in my forties, I donned the lab coat, embracing the scientific wonders of microbiology, biotechnology, and environmental endocrinology.

Today, I bridge the gap between science and spirit, managing business data while building online communities for healing. In this harmonious blend, true well-being blossoms.

Resilience is woven into every fiber of my being. Living with multiple sclerosis hasn't stopped me from embracing life's joys, and a recent epilepsy-induced near-death experience led to the creation of my new workbook, Weaving NDE Threads: Cultivating Meaning and Purpose After Your Near Death Experience. Together, we can untangle the threads of your experience and weave them into a tapestry of newfound meaning and purpose.

My Adverse Childhood Experiences (ACE) score of 10 out of 10 speaks volumes about the childhood trauma I've grappled with, but from the ashes rose resilience. A Million words penned with a trauma-informed therapist, along with daily doses of exercise, healthy meals, meditation, dance, and journaling, have become my armor against life's storms.

About the Creator

And now, I extend my hand not as a healer from afar, but as a fellow warrior. My Harmony Mind Renewal workbook – a 10-day mind detox journey for 1000 individuals – invites you to join me by January 1st, 2025. Let's embark on this path together, where ancient wisdom and modern science unlock the door to mindful living, and uncover practices that resonate deeply with your soul.

My heart yearns for connection. It desires to build RQLRN, a healing community of 1000 people by January 1st, 2025. It longs to share my gifts with the world, embrace lifelong learning, and empower others on their spiritual journeys. This quest began with Harmony Mind Renewal, and now it continues with you.

How can I help?
- Safe Space: You are seen and heard here, embraced in all your unique facets. This space celebrates diversity in backgrounds, beliefs, and identities.
- Systems & Research: I thrive on transforming big-picture ideas into tangible systems, fueled by research and the thrill of discovery.
- Social Connection: Laughter, shared moments, and inspiring connections mend our souls. Let's weave them together.

My story is an open book, its pages filled with challenges overcome and wisdom gleaned. Join me, dear friends, as we paint the next chapter together, one mindful breath at a time.

Reach out. Connect. Heal. Together.

Lots of love,

Raquel René Martin

P.S. Uncover further echoes of my journey in my books, available on Amazon, and explore finding meaning after your own NDE with my new workbook, Weaving NDE Threads.

Nurturing Resilience Quiz

Our "Nurturing Resilience" quiz explores childhood experiences, drawing from the ACE study. It's a legitimate tool for self-reflection and growth, addressing factors beyond ACE, such as discrimination and poverty. Seek professional guidance for a comprehensive evaluation.

References

Felitti, V. J., Anda, R. F., Nordenberg, D., Williamson, D. F., Spitz, A. M., Edwards, V., ... & Marks, J. S. (1998). Relationship of childhood abuse and household dysfunction to many of the leading causes of death in adults: The Adverse Childhood Experiences (ACE) Study. American Journal of Preventive Medicine, 14(4), 245-258. https://doi.org/10.1016/S0749-3797(98)00017-8

Davidson, R. J., Kabat-Zinn, J., Schumacher, J., Rosenkranz, M., Muller, D., Santorelli, S. F., ... & Sheridan, J. F. (2003). Alterations in brain and immune function produced by mindfulness meditation. Psychosomatic Medicine, 65(4), 564–570. https://doi.org/10.1097/01.PSY.0000077505.67574.E3

Hölzel, B. K., Carmody, J., Vangel, M., Congleton, C., Yerramsetti, S. M., Gard, T., ... & Lazar, S. W. (2011). Mindfulness practice leads to increases in regional brain gray matter density. Psychiatry Research: Neuroimaging, 191(1), 36–43. https://doi.org/10.1016/j.pscychresns.2010.08.006

Kabat-Zinn, J. (1994). Wherever you go, there you are: Mindfulness meditation in everyday life. Hyperion.

Siegel, D. J. (2007). The mindful brain: Reflection and attunement in the cultivation of well-being. W. W. Norton & Company.

Brown, K. W., & Ryan, R. M. (2003). The benefits of being present: Mindfulness and its role in psychological well-being. Journal of Personality and Social Psychology, 84(4), 822–848. https://doi.org/10.1037/0022-3514.84.4.822

Davidson, R. J., & McEwen, B. S. (2012). Social influences on neuroplasticity: Stress and interventions to promote well-being. Nature Neuroscience, 15(5), 689–695. https://doi.org/10.1038/nn.3093

References

Lutz, A., Slagter, H. A., Dunne, J. D., & Davidson, R. J. (2008). Attention regulation and monitoring in meditation. Trends in Cognitive Sciences, 12(4), 163–169. https://doi.org/10.1016/j.tics.2008.01.005

Goleman, D., & Davidson, R. J. (2017). Altered traits: Science reveals how meditation changes your mind, brain, and body. Avery.

Van der Kolk, B. A. (2014). The body keeps the score: Brain, mind, and body in the healing of trauma. Viking.

Hanson, R. (2009). Buddha's brain: The practical neuroscience of happiness, love, and wisdom. New Harbinger Publications.

Hölzel, B. K., Lazar, S. W., Gard, T., Schuman-Olivier, Z., Vago, D. R., & Ott, U. (2011). How does mindfulness meditation work? Proposing mechanisms of action from a conceptual and neural perspective. Perspectives on Psychological Science, 6(6), 537–559. https://doi.org/10.1177/1745691611419671

Cozolino, L. (2014). The neuroscience of human relationships: Attachment and the developing social brain (2nd ed.). W. W. Norton & Company.

Gilbert, P. (2010). Compassion focused therapy: Distinctive features. Routledge.

my
mindfulness
practices

○ ....

○ ....

○ ....

○ ....

○ ....

○ ....

○ ....

○ ....

○ ....

○ ....

○ ....

○ ....

journal
entry

journal
entry

journal
entry

journal entry

Connect with Us on Social Media

UNLEASH YOUR CREATIVITY AND SHARE THE LOVE! WE'D BE THRILLED TO SEE HOW YOU BRING YOUR HARMONY MIND RENEWAL JOURNEY TO LIFE. TAG US IN YOUR POSTS AND FOLLOW OUR JOURNEY FOR MORE INSPIRING CONTENT ON YOUTUBE AND TIKTOK.

✺ FOLLOW AND TAG US! ✺

TIKTOK: @RQLRN

YOUTUBE: RQLRN

STAY CONNECTED, GET INSPIRED, AND BECOME PART OF OUR GROWING COMMUNITY!

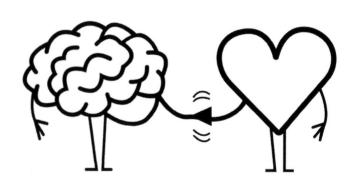

Books
by
RQLRN
Now on Amazon

Weaving NDE Threads:
Cultivating Meaning and Purpose After Near Death Experiences
by Raquel René Martin

A Mystical Account of Seizures and Transcendence
by Raquel René Martin

Your Exclusive Invitation: Welcome to the Harmony Mind Renewal Circle

Embrace this special opportunity designed just for our readers. By scanning the QR code below, you're taking a step toward enriching your mindfulness practice with a community that understands and supports your journey. It's our gift to you—a chance to join the Harmony Mind Renewal Circle and enjoy 10 days of guided connection and personal growth at no cost.

How to Use the QR Code:

1. Open the camera app on your smartphone or QR code scanner.
2. Point your camera at the QR code below and follow the prompt to open your email app.
3. Your email will be pre-addressed with the subject "Join the Harmony Mind Renewal Circle". Feel free to add a personal message if you like!
4. Send the email, and we'll respond with your invitation to the circle.

Made in the USA
Las Vegas, NV
13 January 2024